Free Verse Editions
Edited by Jon Thompson

I Am Not Korean

Song Kyeong-dong

Translated by Brother Anthony of Taizé

Parlor Press
Anderson, South Carolina
www.parlorpress.com

Parlor Press LLC, Anderson, South Carolina, 29621

나는 한국인이 아니다 (I AM NOT KOREAN) © 2016 by [송경동 (Song Kyeong-dong). Originally published in Korea by Changbi Publishers, Inc. English translation © 2025 by An Seonjae (Brother Anthony of Taizé). The English edition is published by Parlor Press in arrangement with Changbi Publishers, Inc.

This book is published with the support of the Literature Translation Institute of Korea (LTI Korea).

Printed in the United States of America
S A N: 2 5 4 - 8 8 7 9

Library of Congress Cataloging-in-Publication Data

Names: Song, Kyŏng-dong, 1967- author. | Anthony, of Taizé, Brother, 1942- translator.
Title: I am not Korean / Song Kyeong-dong ; translated by Brother Anthony of Taizé.
Other titles: Na nŭn Han'gugin i anida. English
Description: Anderson, South Carolina : Parlor Press, 2025. | Summary: "This collection of poetry from social activist and poet Song Kyeong-dong evokes many heroic protests and some tragic incidents, but the poet never loses his sense of humor, and never loses sight of what is worthy of truly human sympathy. Song's poems are records of a heroic commitment to social justice"-- Provided by publisher.
Identifiers: LCCN 2024060730 (print) | LCCN 2024060731 (ebook) | ISBN 9781643175072 (paperback) | ISBN 9781643175089 (pdf) | ISBN 9781643175096 (epub)
Subjects: LCGFT: Poetry.
Classification: LCC PL994.78.K96 N313 2025 (print) | LCC PL994.78.K96 (ebook) | DDC 895.71/5--dc23/eng/20241231
LC record available at https://lccn.loc.gov/2024060730
LC ebook record available at https://lccn.loc.gov/2024060731
978-1-64317-507-2 (paperback)
978-1-64317-508-9 (pdf)
978-1-64317-509-6 (ePub)

2 3 4 5

Book design by David Blakesley.

Parlor Press, LLC is an independent publisher of scholarly and trade titles in print and multimedia formats. This book is available in paperback and ebook formats from Parlor Press on the World Wide Web at https://www.parlorpress. com or through online and brick-and-mortar bookstores. For submission information or to find out about Parlor Press publications, write to Parlor Press, 3015 Brackenberry Drive, Anderson, South Carolina, 29621, or email editor@parlorpress.com.

Contents

Introduction

What kind of world do you live in?

I live in the Republic of Korea, a divided country where confrontation and conflict have been repeated under a 'truce' for over seventy years.

Although I escaped the chains of military dictatorship more than thirty years ago, I still live in the Republic of Korea, where countless people must pour out into the streets and squares for minimal democracy.

I believe that the top 10% of the privileged class own 46.5% of the total national income and earn nearly five times their share, while the bottom 50% receive 16.0% of the total national income and earn less than one-third of their share. We live in an extremely unequal society.

I naturally became a seditious poet in this breathless land.

The beautiful flowers, birds, wind, and sea could not sing and had to live along with the people who were kicked out, such as street vendors, evictees, and laid-off workers. While crying out for freedom of expression in press, publication, association, and freedom of conscience and thought, I had to shout out not to arrest those who were being taken away by public power. I had to hold my breath while looking at the people who had climbed to high places in the distance, such as steel towers, factory chimneys, or railings on bridges, to protest. In the process of resisting, I had to cry out in front of the pitiful souls who were beaten to death, hanged themselves, or burned to death. We had to shout out not to trample on the rights of minorities, such as the disabled, queer, non-regular female migrant workers who cry out in the face of social disaster and discrimination. "You must not cross this line." "This is a dangerous place." I had to scream like a canary trapped in a deep coal mine with the miners at a site where all human dignity, rights, and justice were being trampled.

But what kind of world do you live in?

Even in the midst of a terrible ecological and climate crisis where even the sustainability of the planet is being challenged, the impending war for profit and exploitation of rights is still not over in many parts of the world, and the descendants of past fascism reappear without shame in various parts of the world. A time when the present and future of all humans and nature are brutally trampled for the unlimited monopoly of multinational capital.

What kind of world are we living in?

I wrote these poems because I wanted to ask you a question.

Song Kyeong-dong
July 2024, across the sea

I Am Not Korean

Song Kyeong-dong
Translated by Brother Anthony

In my early twenties, when I was just discovering literature, there was a poet who inspired me and helped me break out of the egg.* She was Nikki Giovanni, the Black American woman poet, who wrote:

> I really hope no white person ever has cause
> to write about me
> because they never understand
> Black love is Black wealth and they'll
> probably talk about my hard childhood
> and never understand that
> all the while I was quite happy"
>
> —from "Nikki-Rosa" in *Black Feeling, Black Talk, Black Judgment*

Dreaming of a world in which such dignity was allowed to anyone became the path for my writing to follow. It was a real revolution, the realization that a world was coming where all beings would be wondrous with their own truth alone, where all ordinary people, without high and low, without comparison, would be great and dignified in themselves. I reckoned that the "association, in which the free development of each is the condition for the free development of all" that Marx had spoken of in the *Communist Manifesto* (Chapter 2) was no different from that.

I am glad to be for the first time in the country of Nikki Giovanni, who gave me inspiration for the way true literature should follow. I am glad to be in the country where, in May 1886, a general strike aimed at obtaining an eight-hour working day at the Haymarket in Chicago was crushed by police gunfire, giving birth to the "International Workers' Day" on May 1. Ever since my early twenties, my birthday has been celebrated, not on September

---

* "I Am Not Korean" was presented at the 2018 Brooklyn Book Festival on 15 September 2018 for a special event on Korean literature and later published in *Korean Literature Now*, vol. 41, Autumn, 2018. https://kln.or.kr/features/coverfeaturesView.do?bbsIdx=658. Used by permission.

15 but on May 1, the day of solidarity of workers and peoples all over the world. I remember how, in 2008, at the time of the struggle of the female "dispatch" workers in Kiryung Electronics, who were earning just ten won more than the legal minimum wage in Korea, when people went to the US to bring the struggle directly to Sirius Satellite Radio, for whom they were working, citizens of the United States came to their assistance. I also remember how, in 2010, in the struggle against Colt-Coltech, which produced one-third of the world's best guitars, such as Ibanez, Fender and Gibson, after they tried to lay off workers in Korea, friends brought their struggle to that year's NAMM show being held in Anaheim. Tom Morello of the rock group 'RATM' (Rage Against The Machine) said, "Guitars should not be produced at the cost of workers' blood and sweat. If multinational capital is trying to exploit labor, the struggle of labor against it should also be done on a multinational level." "Then he dedicated the song "Worldwide Rebel Song" in solidarity, for which I am grateful.

Above all, I am glad to be here in New York where, in the fall of 2011, faced with the absurdity of one percent of multinational financial capital accounting for fifty percent of total social wealth, "We are the 99%" and "Occupy Wall Street" emerged. I was thinking about the "comrades" of Zuccotti Park at that time, as I was on the run for my work planning the "Hope bus for a world without layoffs and temporary workers" against the restructuring of neoliberalism in Korea. The 1955 bus boycott in Montgomery against racial discrimination after the arrest of Rosa Parks had been big news in Korea, and now, on five occasions, workers and citizens from all over Korea spontaneously chartered buses to take them to Busan in support of workers at Hanjin Heavy Industries and Construction, who were striking in protest at layoffs, including a sit-in on top of a forty-meter-high crane. At the time, my soul was not lonely even though I was shut up in solitary confinement in a tiny prison cell. Some days I was sitting together in Zuccotti Park, or in a corner of some Arabian plaza where the Jasmine Revolution was taking place, either marching or shaking my fist against monopolistic conglomerates or against some dictator. The world may seem to be isolated, but the world's dreamers are all one.

In early November 2016, as we set up a "Park Geun-hye-must-resign camping village" in central Seoul's Gwanghwamun Plaza close to the presidential mansion, in a proposal I dreamed that our plaza might expand "like Zuccotti Park with its dream of '99% against 1%' which occupied Wall Street in New York, the center of the world's economy, in September 2011, or like Tabriz Square in Egypt's Cairo which saw the start of the 'Arab

Spring' that same year. Only the direct democracy of workers and common citizens gathered in our squares and streets would be able to properly judge the Park Geun-hye regime and bring Korean society to a new stage of democracy."

So we are linked. We are all connected in opposition to this unjust world, which is constantly trying to turn each and every person into an alienated isolated individual, person and person, group and group, by borders, poor and rich, powerful and powerless, by products, by money. It is the task of literature to imagine such organic relationships and a shared world, and constantly restore the truth of buried events and relationships. So, while we engage together with the concrete tasks and struggles against specific injustices and contradictions here-and-now, never stopping to ask fundamental questions, dreaming about a deeper, more robust "long-lasting future" must be the permanent victory and permanent defeat for literature. Not a literature that offers ordinary explanations or difficult commentaries on a world that is already dead and gone; it has to be a literature that often despairs and and collapses as it pursues the new language of a world that has not yet come. It has to be a literature that brings together the fruits of despair and hope to create another rare form of life.

To put it briefly, it has to be a literature that dreams seditious dreams going beyond this unjust world in which the total assets of 225 multinational capitalists total more than the total annual income of 2.5 billion of the world's poor. In which the sales of each of the world's top one hundred conglomerates are greater than the total exports of one hundred and twenty poor countries, while the amount of speculative financial capital flowing in and out each year is sixty-five times greater than the total value of goods and services produced by the people of the entire world, so that it has to be the universal duty of contemporary literature to go beyond this present century of fraud, monopoly and violence, and dream again. It has to be a literature that reacts more sensitively and shudders before the present day's barbarism, where in order to achieve monopolistic wealth and privileges, nature is destroyed, nuclear weapons are produced and possessed, ethnic groups are discriminated against and exploited, wars are waged, all public goods are privatized, all areas of value necessary for human life are marketized and commercialized, while distorting history to block resistance and revolution and to colonize all areas of the press, publishing, education, and culture.

We need to remember that good literature has always revived and emerged like a miracle on abandoned frontiers or hidden frontlines. We need to remember that the beautiful literary tradition that we must follow has never flourished in the antechambers of dictators, the siderooms of opportunists, or at the overflowing tables of capital. Those are affectations and fallacies that cannot become the target of freedom and that have to avoid mentioning freedom. So long as all the misery and suffering of the world has not ended, it is sinful or disrespectful to be too readily discouraged and we should sing as much as possible about the possibility of yet greater hope and social transformation.

Specifically, there seems to be one thing that Korean writers and conscientious American literary people have to do together. That is to overcome the division of the Korean peninsula and unite our efforts for peace. Once again the United States is not helping Korea. The US, that 'monster state,' which since the start of the modern era has been responsible for so many wars and disputes, must reflect deeply on its past imperialistic history, which it has to reject so that American society can be reformed. Fortunately, summit talks have recently been held between North and South Korea as well as North Korea and the United States. For the first time, there have been promises of a "Peace Treaty" for the Korean Peninsula to replace the "North Korea-US Armistice Agreement," together with the lifting of various economic sanctions and an end to large-scale military exercises, the provision of economic support, and other forms of exchange and cooperation. I hope that we can combine forces so that this wave of peace can become an irresistible trend.

Literature is the conviction that "if capitalism armed with imperialism achieved globalization by force, we will attain it with the very old-style conventional weapons of love and compassion." That literature "will use the palpitating human heart as a detonator and so cover the human world more completely than any nuclear shield."*

Brooklyn, New York
15 September 2018

---

* From my doggerel poem, "Butterfly Effect."

I Am Not Korean

A Noble Inheritance

Whenever workers give up their lives,
saying they hope the world will change even if they have to die,
as if they have nothing else left to give,

The conservative media say,
"Don't exploit death!"

Peru's mountain railway up to celestial Lake Titicaca
started construction in 1870 and took 30 years to complete.
During that construction work more than 2,000 workers died.
It runs for thirteen hours through perpetual snows without a single station,
stopping just once for twenty minutes.

I can think of people taking a train,
but that's like riding on the biers of 2,000 corpses.
Don't exploit death?
If society does not take our lives as something to be exploited
there will be no special mourning for someone's death.

There are surprisingly few stations in life
where we can choose to get off for ourselves.

Mother's Native Tongue

From the moment we were born
we were all 'people from Beolgyo'
but for many years Mother
was just 'the woman from Yeocheon.'

Apart from that, she had no name
and it was only after I started school that at some point
in my school records
she became 'Ms. Yi Cheong-ja.'

She ate alone by the kitchen range
and always came following on at the very back,
scurrying along with something perched on her head.
She came in after everyone else was in bed,
then would slip out quietly
at dawn.

Mother
was like someone from another country
who'd been borrowed
and would have to be sent back one day,

The nearest, most remote country,
where many conches and clams grew.
But we were never once able to hear
Mother's native tongue.

The Day I Had an MRI

No matter how well a building is built,
I can see its inner skeleton as if I'm wearing X-ray glasses.

Rusty rebars, twisted pipes,
loose fittings, warped window frames,
thin wires, dented ducts, pebbles
buried in the concrete, here and there
even traces of piss, I see them all.

I try wearing other glasses,
it's no good, they're vivid even with my eyes shut.

Choi, whose toe was crushed by an H beam,
Ahn, who lost an eye to a grinder,
Kim, who pierced his hand,
Ko, who was done in alone by an elevator,
Won, who fell backward off scaffolding,
Park, who died pinned under a machine
after hitting the ground three times,
Wang, who got stuck to a welding line on a rainy day.

It wasn't horizontal,
the finishings are not perfect,
that spot ought to be reinforced,
more than wretched wages, a broken body,
a properly finished job lingers before the eyes.

A worker at forty.

Ode to Pliers

I received a photo sent by Cha Kwang-ho,
after he had spent more than two hundred days at the top of the factory chimney
of Star Chemicals in Gumi industrial park, North Gyeongsang Province,
showing rectangles stacked in layers of multiple shape and color,
gorgeous colors like Van Gogh's sunflowers.
I asked him if he had been painting pictures up there, it looked very beautiful,
and he replied that he had been piling up plastic bottles filled with his piss
to use as weapons when they tried to dislodge him from the chimney.
Depending on what he ate that day, the pattern of the frozen bottles changed,
producing such beautiful work.
Even great things are also material, he said.

At about the same time, Lee Chang-geun, who had already been living for three months
at the top of the chimney at Ssangyong Motors in Pyeongtaek,
asked me if I knew what he felt most grateful for after he climbed the 70-meter chimney.
He said it was a pair of wire-cutting pliers. Having pliers at 2 in the morning
he'd been able to cut the barbed wire and make his way down the chimney.
He chatted on about how the greatest material made by man
was those pliers. And after he climbed up the chimney,
what enabled him to live was specific materials and phenomena,
but he was especially grateful to the wind
that always gave him 'labor,'
tearing his plastic tent.
sprinkling him with soot from the chimney or bringing clouds of dust.

People who have worked in the most precipitous places know:
material is so much more precious than ideas,
labor makes people so human.

The Air Club

When Kim Jin-suk broke the Guinness record with his hundreds of days of a high-altitude sit-in on crane number 85 in Busan's Yeongdo Hanjin Heavy Industries, Park Jeom-gyu, who has many good ideas, suggested creating a "High Altitude Club." His plan was that they should carefully select just one hundred people who, unable to live on level ground, had gone climbing up to a high altitude.

During the irregular workers' struggle at Kiryung Electronics I climbed up onto a mechanical digger, so I naturally assumed I would be a member, but I was excluded. When I protested that I had even fallen off while demonstrating and been taken to hospital, I was told that I had only gone less than 5 meters up and that it was considered a travesty for a "High Altitude Club." The fellow who climbed the highest was a temporary worker in Hyundai Hysco who had gone up 130 meters. If I was dissatisfied, I could organize a "Low Altitude Club."

The reason for failing another candidate was really ridiculous. He had been hanging from the railings of a Han River bridge as an irregular at Bupyeong GM-Daewoo, then jumped into the river. "Hey, I covered more than 30 meters, so why exclude me?" The answer was amazing: that had merely been empty air, not a high altitude. If he was dissatisfied, he could organize a separate "Air Club," and everyone chortled.

Thus times that could not be considered without tears of blood came together, creating a club of beautiful people that had never been able to exist on earth before.

Poet and Convict

In the morning of the day I was to receive the Cheon Sang-Byeong Poetry Award
I was standing in a courtroom at the Seoul Central District Court,
waiting to receive my sentence.

Justice on the one hand,
illegality on the other. Fortunately,
while the fine was three million won, the prize money was five million,
so justice won in part.

In the afternoon of the day I heard I was to receive
the Shin Dong-yeop Literary Award,
I heard the overwhelming news that
an arrest warrant had finally been issued for me.

When I go somewhere to receive an award,
I feel ashamed all day long, as though I'm out of place,
but when I go to receive a sentence
my heart is brimming, I feel so blameless.

I hope I shall receive a lot more summonses
and arrest warrants.
Rather than writing some great poem,
I would not mind committing some broader, larger crime.

Physical Philosophy

Once more I was carted off for investigation,
and in holding cell 13 of Busan Public Prosecutors' Office
someone had written on the wall: "I've survived four years, so
why shouldn't I manage another two and a half?
Friend, make your body really fit to go! See you again!"

Does that mean even perfecting magical ways of contracting space
so as never to be caught again,
building muscles that can snap handcuffs or ropes?
It certainly doesn't seem to be about making one's body healthy
so as to become some kind of worker.

What kind of body should I make for myself?
I've made various plans of action
but I never once thought concretely about my body.
It's hard doing ten press-ups,
five sit-ups are too much for me.

Green thoughts behind bars,
wondering what action I can do with this kind of body,
when workout turns into a brain sport,
and whether I too should make my body 'really fit' to go out?

The Sea's Interrogation Room

I hear there are people who work at night,
waves breaking beneath their feet, as if calming me.
I say I know nothing about it.

Tonight, too, there are turning lines, I hear,
waves from all sides opening mouths, asking me things.
I say I do not know, do not know and longer.

Tonight, too, people are being dragged away, I hear,
waves rising abruptly, up to my eyes,
so what about it?
I say that now I only want to forget it all.

Still all at a loss
as the waves strike my face,
I ask, What did I do wrong?
I just want to weep, rolling like gravel.

I pursue, saying I was a labor activist for 20 years.
On a shore I visited without any dreams
that was the waves' night-long interrogation

A Back Yard

After all, nobody's coming up here!
For several days I threw cigarette ash out onto the snow
in front of the temple dormitory then, disliking the sight,
covered it with a pile of snow scuffed up by my fur boots.
All my life long, that's what I've done,
lightly covering over mistakes,
living as an opportunist.

So long as it can't be seen, it's okay.
Standing on the sill of the door,
I shot piss this way and that.
It pierced holes like bullet marks
that I covered over with snow, so that the clerk
coming to work early in the morning would not see them.

Many times I've said that the world should be overturned,
but before that, maybe what's inside me should be overturned first?
As I clear away the dirty snow
I feel a spade stabbing down in my breast.

Another Story

Postmodern, postterritorialization, postcolonialism, poststructuralism . . .
words I used to think of using 'post-'.
Today I've been shelling soy beans with a thresher.

To the regular boom of the moving machine
the fresh beans came rattling out, substantial and solid,
filling the new sacks.
Saying we're bound up together is just a set phrase,
how much longer are we going to be confined in old relationships?
Surely casting off our old skin and being born anew
is something really valuable?

As they pour down, rustling,
today the beans are new.

The Day I Learned a Lesson

After I fell from a mechanical digger
I crawled back up, saying I wasn't going to the hospital,
and spent seven hours in the tent,
a piece of wood wrapped in a handkerchief between my teeth.
Detectives from the Intelligence Division came running belatedly,
worried they might lose their prey,
and remained lingering around the digger

At midnight, preceded and followed by close vigilance,
I was taken to hospital in secret. My heel bone
was broken in bits like a biscuit.
It was so swollen they said they could not operate,
just gave me a painkiller, then I had to endure a whole day.
I was sorrier still at not having been able to continue the sit-in to the end
it hurt more than I could endure,
but they said I had done my best.
Unable to sacrifice a school record or anything like other people,
belatedly I had at least sacrificed one foot,
and I promised that once I got out
I would be properly active.

But the goddam worst was still to come,
hiding black inside my body.
As part of the sit-in protest I had been fasting on and off
and now, for the first time in twenty days
the order came for me to empty my bowels
so I struggled onto my wheelchair alone and tried several times
but my stool, hard as a cannonball, would not come out
and my blood-gorged legs ached as if the stitches would snap.
Then once opened up, like a stake pulled from the ground,
my behind, torn open, refused to close.
Oh, that struggle was a first for me,
that night spent writhing all alone, nose running, tears flowing.

For the first time
I came to learn what action is.
Real action is not done with the mouth

but with the behind,
it's not done by a noble soul
it's done by an aching, messy body.
As my anus was torn, that's what I learned.

Ever since that day
I have never been able to say too glibly
that action should be done with one's whole body.

(In Korean, 'hakmun' means 'learning,' 'hangmun' means 'anus,' but when
pronounced they sound the same.)

The Last Leaf

*When I read "The Last Leaf" or "The Yellow Handkerchief" as a
child, I was happy.*

Even though I become senile after returning from four years of prison
or an old guy dessiccated by TB,
there is a hope that maybe someone or other
will hang a yellow handkerchief round a tree
or draw a last leaf for me,

Of course, my youth was also beautiful.
For I saw countless yellow handkerchiefs
saying that everyone should live together
fluttering tied to factory guardrails,
fluttering from the window of a watchtower at a demolition site,
fluttering from Han River bridges and from cranes,
fluttering from CC camera supports.

For I saw so many last leaves
saying we have to live for one another
on the iron skeletons of buildings' vertical exterior walls,
on the pipes of empty union offices,
hanging themselves on the flagpole at the front gate of factories they were
     fired from,
burning themselves in front of Hyatt Hotel on Seoul's Nam-san,
self-immolating on the overpass above Seoul Station.

Under those yellow handkerchiefs,
before those last leaves,
I saw so many people weeping,
so my life's expectations were not in vain.

Six Summonses

I come home late one night
and my wife hands me a bunch of mail—
summonses from Jongno Police Station, Yeongdeungpo Police Station,
Seocho Police Station, Namdaemun Police Station and Seoul Central
    District Court,
six summonses from various locations,
on the same day at the same time. Should I tell Guinness World Records?

One for the day when I protested
at the Eulchiro crossroads with non-regular workers from Kiryung Electronics,
one for the day when I protested
before the Supreme Court with the workers dismissed from Ssangyong Motors,
one for the day when I demonstrated
in front of the National Assembly with non-regular workers from LGU +
    SK Broadband,
one charging me with sedition for the sit-in protest on top of the
    advertising towers
in front of the Central Post Office in Myeongdong,
and one for going with everyone in front of the Blue House,
while the last was a summons for a trial related to the Seweol Ferry
    memorial ceremony.

By our standards, those were
a press conference, a memorial service that needs no reporting,
cultural events, expressions of compassion,
of conscience being unable to look the other way,
of solidarity for a sustainable society.

By their standards, they were
the organization of an unauthorized assembly,
infringements of the law on assemblies and demonstrations,
refusal to disperse, slogan chanting, picketing, producing excessive
    noise, trespassing,
acts of violence, etc., specific illegal, criminal activities,
obstructing government officials, general obstruction of traffic.

Intending to cook braised beef
in order to finally get high marks from our kid,
I quickly set about boiling down soy sauce . . . .
it was the day I'd bought plenty of quail eggs.

The only people who want to meet me
right now,
are the nation's police and prosecutors,
so recently I've changed my favorite song to Lee Seon-hee's "Meeting."
It was the day I'd just managed to be released on bail
after being sentenced at the first trial to two years in prison
for organizing the Hope Bus in 2011, not long ago.
I liked the lyrics:
"You say two years? I cannot refuse."
Then it gets even better.
"Will I ever see a day as beautiful as this in all my life?"
And what about the next phrase?
"You are a gift on my life's hard road."

With my cooking
I hope my child's heart that's been turning from me
will turn back again,
it's good and tasty.
What?
The braised beef?
My life?

An Order

We're moving house and there's no end of chaos in the household.
In my dreams two big snakes
disappear into the bamboo grove out back.

Though I know it's superstition, if I don't catch them at the start
the spell might never end.
Every night I crept into Mother's dreams.

Having lurked hidden for several days
I caught one after a desperate fight
but in the end I missed the other.
Now it's impatient to appear.

Then one afternoon I fell asleep.
Do you think you're going to catch me?
Mother turned into a python, slipped over the wall
and slithered into the bamboo grove.

I'll need about a thousand years
before I understand Mother's order.

Mundingi's Family Story

Once Mother had finally taken control of the household
after she passed seventy,
Father slowly became for her "that Mundingi."

The third daughter of my youngest sister,
Mi-yeon, who lives with them, learned that word
went to the nursery school and firmly, brightly,
pronounced it several times.
"My grandfather is . . . Mundingi."

My sister, hearing of that and
feeling it would not do, corrected her at every opportunity:
"Mi-yeon, dear, Grandfather is not Mundingi, he's Gabriel. Do you understand?"
Perhaps it had an effect because she was such an intelligent child.
Some time later, the child boasted brightly
about her grandfather to the nursery-school teachers:
"My grandfather, he's not Mundingier, he's Gabriel."

So all the members of the family reached an agreement
never to use the word Mundingi.
Now my sister, who will soon be forty,
observes sharp-eared Mi-yeon
and whispers to her like a star in the night sky:
With the passage of time, even unforgettable wounds
clear up a little.

* "Mundingi" or "Mundungi" is a belittling name used formerly to designate peo-
ple with Hansen's disease. Older Koreans often use it in an affectionate manner,
as a nickname for someone close to them who sometimes irritates or contradicts
them. The poet adds a note: "It refers to my deeply wounded family story. Please
forgive me."

A Stammerer

In my youth I used to stutter.
Please go further out into the world.
I used to spend half the day biting my short-rooted tongue, telling it
it should be able to roll around like pebbles on a beach.
I rolled my tongue round, rr, rr, rr, a thousand times,
until suddenly it was sunset.

That short tongue was the height of my little soul.
I acquired the strength to reject entirely the sounds
of the words of supreme domination, violence and progress.
I was alert to all kinds of slick words and learned
that in the world there are far more sorrows that cannot be spoken,
pains that still cannot be spoken,
words that cannot emerge.

Still now, I watch myself
as I practice beautiful words when I'm alone.
The word I most wanted to pronounce, 'Greetings,'
after stammering,
there are still so many words I cannot speak,
I'm happy, no time to be weary.

Dawn Snack

A hymn to youth 1

Around the age of twenty, I wanted to be a mine worker.
I duly went to the employment agency in Eulchiro 5ga,
with a few old clothes in a bag, nothing else.
I intended to say that I had made a mess of my life
and bury myself deep underground,

After paying the brokerage fee of thirty thousand won
I had twenty thousand won left.
While we waited for the van that was due at dawn
six of us took a room in an unfamiliar inn.
Surely we weren't being sold to be sent to a desert island?
Clutching tight the twenty thousand won in my pocket,
I stayed awake all night, then at misty dawn
stealthily crept away.

That dawn, standing in a hole-in-the-wall store
in the printing-shop lane in Eulchiro
I gulped down a whole bottle of soju
and as a snack to accompany it I was lucky to get
three freshly boiled eggs.
How could I ever forget
that strong, salty taste?

A Disease Worse than TB

A hymn to youth 2

While I did day-labor found through an employment agent whose office
was a converted communal bath in the basement of an inn
down an alley among the hardware stores in Jongro 2ga,
I lived in a room I rented for a hundred thousand won a month.
The guy I shared with was a professional card-sharper.
His rule was never to bet more than fifty thousand won at a time
and only to work for two weeks in a month to avoid suspicion,
while never staying in any one place for more than three months.
The bowls of a boiled half-chicken with rice costing five thousand won
he sometimes bought for me tasted really good.
I would stay up all night reading books and writing poems.
He used to tell me: Don't live like me, make good.
It was only on the day he left that he finally confessed
he had TB.
That day, after he'd left, for the first time
I hung out my clammy bedding on a line on the sunny roof of the inn.
We were even, because I couldn't tell him that I suffered from a disease
worse than TB, called loneliness,
and instead simply wished him well:
Good luck! Don't get caught!

The Difference between Salt and Natrium

A hymn to youth 3

While working as a carpenter on new apartment blocks,
one of the hardest parts
is going down to work on the shuttering for the basement
under a blazing midsummer's sun.

With the added heat coming from the hardening concrete
it's like being sent into a high-temperature sauna,
so we go rushing in wearing only panties and a nail bag,
each holding a nail puller, then emerge again,
as it's hard for anyone to endure more than 30 minutes in there,
and I can't forget the rough briny taste of the handful of salt
spotted with black
they used to give us as we came running out
to prevent dehydration.

And as for Guro Industrial Park,
in the factories making aluminum foil,
as I worked, steamed like dumplings in a steamer
they would hand out round, white tablets of natrium,
utterly insipid with neither elegance nor taste.

I Can't Forget These Songs

While we were building a new factory on 490 acres of reclaimed land
in Dokgot-ri, Daesan-myeon, Seosan-gun, we were living like so
    much trash.
The rebars were wet, the toolboxes were wet,
the blueprints, the working clothes and the welding rods were all wet.
One afternoon when even our hearts were wet,
taking shelter in one remote corner of a warehouse,
I was singing sad songs when the guy in charge of stores
asked why I was being so miserable, told me to get out.
I asked why he was being so nasty, turned my back,
and felt a Bang! on the back of my head,
fell down, got up, only to receive a full swing in the face,
the skin split from the side of the nose down to my lips.
four teeth were shattered.
That was the price of one song.

Those songs remain unforgotten, still now.
"You, woman weeding the bean field, your hempen jacket is soaked.
You have so many sorrows that you sow tears at every step!"
The song contest held once a week in Gwangju prison's juvenile
    detention block
with five sponge cakes and two cans of white peaches for the winner:
Ku Chang-mo's "Green Firewood" that used to be played
as reveille in Jeonju juvenile detention center at 6 am:
 "My heart was so sensitive to your feelings
that it came to you as restraint."
How should a song be sung so that it smells rusty?
Jang Hyeon, or Bae Ho, or Kim Chu-ja,
comrades' hoarse songs heard here and there
during night shifts at work,
Bang bang bang, a sound of hammering echoing in the night,
welding sparks that fell from the sky like fireworks displays,
Quitting time did not come readily,
even after we had sung all the songs we knew.

Time has passed, and at 6 in the morning
in Seoul City Hall Square, Kiryung Electronics workers climbed to the top

of a 25-meter-high light tower, "Forward!
Break through the exploitation of subcontracted workers"
as they called for solidarity with the abolition of non-regular workers,
while far away in Geoje Island
looking up at a companion who had climbed alone
35 meters up a transmission tower with a view of the sea.
Workers from Daewoo Shipbuilding puming their fists and singing:
"Don't blame days gone by,
don't swear at youth gone past,

* * *

we all share a common fate, anyway."

"Separation's too long, sorrow's too long,
the time spent standing in line is too long,
the dried-up Milky Way has been melted by tears,
put a horse-block on this chest and that,
you woman beckoning."

At midnight on the hundredth day
of a high-up sit-in on crane 85
where a friend had hanged himself,
for Kim Jin-suk, who had gone back up,
after placing candles in a heart shape beneath the darkened crane,
as I watch the hundredth-day song contest by
old workers Hanjin Heavy Industry,
still I wander the streets, thinking that
for us, there will be other love songs.

Concerning Ladders

I've climbed up a lot of ladders in my life.
In my childhoos they were mainly wooden ladders,
ladders made of rotten boards ripped from fish crates,
ladders where one or two ancient steps had collapsed,
sometimes made of knotted wood gathered on a hillside.

Picturesque crooked ladders,
ladders made of metal bars cut and welded together,
dangerous ladders where the welded parts had grown old and fallen off,
ladders where the Wooden Age and the Iron Age
met awkwardly as iron pipes linked to wooden parts,
ladders where the spaces between the steps soon varied,
no matter how thick the wire used to bind them was,
ladders attached to tall factory chimneys,
ladders that my hands stuck to in winter,
ladders balanced precariously like a railroad track in midair
where I risked my life every time I had to cross them trembling.

Ladders I had to climb up with a hod on my back,
ladders I had to climb up with a pail on my back,
ladders I had to climb up to lay pipes,
ladders I had to climb up to make ducts,
ladders I had to climb up to make ceilings,
ladders I had to climb up to install equipment.

Ladders in the 'chicken-coop' village at Guro industrial complex,
the upstairs room in a shack I had to enter through a square hole
after climbing up a shoulder-wide right-angled ladder,
the ladder that led from that room up to the storage loft,
ladders leaning like sentries against every house
so that people could climb up to tend
the lettuce in styrofoam, the chilis in crates, the tomatoes in
abandoned buckets
on the roof of ever chicken-coop house,
some slender, others stocky,
each ladder different.

Shouting, all at once,
iron ladders workers used to cross over factory walls
to save a moment,
ladders of desperation leading to some small nest above a CC camera pylon,
up onto the railings coated with grease of a bridge over the Han River,
up some remote transmission tower,
up an advertising tower where a dazzling light show gleamed,
up a watchtower or a shelter,
the hearts that had fallen
somewhere far below them.

I even longed to climb a ladder leading to a higher rank
that they said existed, the size of a needle's eye,
although now all that's past.
But when, in order to see the stars better,
to get a bit closer to the warm sunshine,
to build a pretty house for myself,
to pick sweet persimmons, apples and pears,
to take down a book from the very top shelf,
to help some tiny cat unable to get down from the roof,
to take good photos,
to draw a good picture,
when will I ever own a ladder as beautiful as that?

Nation: Reasons for Disqualification

After being married for over fifteen years,
I find everything is growing older,
the TV flickering,
the video head worn away by the cleaner,
the gas range's knobs dropped off
so I have to struggle with pliers to use it.

But what has not grown old is promises,
the promise to live together until our black hair has turned white as snow,
the promise we all would visit there and lend a helping hand
and swallowed down a bowl of rib soup,
the 'When are you coming?' phone call,
the 'Where are you?' phone call,
the 'Have you found the kid?' phone call,
the 'Yes' phone call,
the 'When did you say you were coming home?' phone call,
the phone call hung up without a word.

But still, reckoning I have to avoid total breakdown,
sometimes I go out to a park and firmly take
a photo of our triangular family alliance that was never asked for,
in a nation that merely notes our complaints with no after-service,
without ever complaining,
little by little I grow older.

Private Materialism

One teacher told me:
If you're overly inclined toward public life
without enough private life,
then you'll die.

An older friend I often used to meet told me:
You must reduce your talk about social activism and increase
private conversation by at least seventy percent,
otherwise, all your relationships will wither and die.

One who often consulted fortune-tellers told me:
You were born as a tree
but with not enough water in your fate
you'll always live a thirsty life.

What with private life, and thus
no energy left to resist with relations or
historical, political life,
one lonesome evening

The times in life when I come to realize that
only win or lose,
only what can or cannot be achieved
is not the whole of life.

I Longed to Wear a Hat

After buying a pair of hiking boots for twenty thousand won
from a late-night street stall near Wonju Bus Terminal,
I hesitated in front of a hat seller.
I've never had a hat I treasured.
I wanted to have my hair bleached or permed
but went on living with just tangled hair.

The first hats I wore were no good.
The hat worn for military training in middle and high school,
that only had to be worn straight like a military cap,
then once I was a worker, the safety helmets stinking of sweat
I would pick up at random and wear on the job,
or the skull hat like a wrestler's worn to keep off the cold,
eyes, nose and mouth alone exposed.

I dreamed of jogging or cycling
wearing a nice sports hat,
of hiking up far-off mountains
wearing a cloche or a trapper,
of going to some remote seashore
wearing a boater or a panama, white with a wavy brim,
all remote fantasies.

The head of Kim Tae-hwan with the brains spurting out,
crushed by the wheel of a strike-breaking cement truck;
the back of welder Ha Jung-geun's head smashed open
with a fire extinguisher by the Pohang Taehwa riverside police;
the heads of the farmers Jeon Yong-cheol and Hong Deok-pyo
beaten with clubs in Yeouido Park;
heavy heads weighed down with that kind of story.

Still now, I would like to own
a lightweight hat capable of being swept off by the wind,
a happy hat capable of a cheerful wink, of laughing out loud,
a hat that looks cheeky or chic,
a nomad's hat I can light-heartedly leave behind,
... but no matter where I look
there's not a trace
of the kind of hat I want to wear.

A Precious Day

Spending the Winter at Guijeong-sa Temple

I worked all morning, digging a path through snowdrifts with a big shovel
then, hungering for red persimmons dangling capped with snow,
I used a long bamboo pole and filled a basket with persimmons.
The three days' snowfall finally stopped and the sun came out
so I did some laundry and hung it up.
I climbed onto the roof of the temple kitchen
and repaired the antenna of the flickering TV
for the old woman who gave me three temple meals every day,
then changed the broken light bulb in the shed, dozed briefly,
and when I woke up, it was evening.

Regretting that the day was already nearly over,
I placed a snow-covered chair under the eaves of the monks' dormitory, sat there
and asked the trees standing black with white snow piled on every gaunt branch
whether they did not feel lonely, exposed to rain and snow in one spot all
      their lives.
I murmured to myself: Today there is really no moon, no stars, no sound
      of wind,
and reflected vaguely that I had seen the crescent moon a few days before
so it must have grown to a half-moon since then
and when it was full moon, it would be a little brighter,
then sighed at the thought that I should write a blood-stained poem for
      Mun Gi-ju,
Han Sang-gyun and Bok Gi-seong who on this cold winter's day
were protesting at the top of a transmission tower at Ssangyong Motors
      in Pyeongtaek,
for Choi Byeong-seung and Cheon Ui-bong on a transmission tower at Hyundai
      Motors in Ulsan,
for Hong Jong-in suspended from the elevated entrance to Yoosung Enterprise
      in Asan,
as well as Jeong Hong-geun and Kim Jae-ju from Jeonbuk Express on a pylon in
      Jeonju City.

Unable to sleep, though the sun has set and the night is dark,
I turn the pages of "The Philosophy of Life" without understanding it,

then, scan the much easier "Record of Linji,"
since my topic needs reflection rather than enlightenment,
I read "Eco-feminism,"
then, flip through George Orwell's "Why I Write,"
since I feel that writing is the only thing I have left,
and as I feel I should not lose sight of the concrete, after all,
I read "Crazy Like US: The Globalization of the American Psyche"
then suddenly wonder if the heater left burning to stop the pipes freezing
    in the washroom
isn't overheating, so hurry across to turn it off, wearing only my
    winter underwear,
and glance up at the distant moonlight,
thinking that one more precious day is over
and will not return.

I Refuse to Say Anything

Told that if I did not present myself on receiving the fourth summons,
an arrest warrant would be issued,
I reluctantly paid a visit to Namdaemun Police Station.
"A total of four charges, I suppose you'll say nothing?"
"No!"

Stealthily glancing at
the diary on the investigator's desk,
I see seven names written with the date of their summons,
all familiar friends,
it seems they've been living it up.
He even asks about my friends by name:
"What is your relationship with X?"
"I refuse to say anything,"
I will say nothing of
my youth,
my streets,
my anguish.
Shall I call it a coincidence?
Through the half-open window on the fourth floor,
without any repentance,
the human rights activist Myeong Sook, my frequent accomplice,
is protesting against the ban on the Queer Festival.
The sound of her voice barking into a mike at the front gate
rings out shrill.
Life all seems like a dream.

"Finally, is all you have told us true?"
"Yes!"
"Do you have anything you want to add?"
"Nothing"
"Are you going to refuse to be fingerprinted?"
"Yes!"
I do not want to say anything more
about this insulting world.

Dogma

Now I do not want
to tell you honestly
anything about what I feel.
I hate the thought of telling you
about how I too longed for a sunny spot,
about times when I felt like collapsing in confusion.
I do not want to reveal how sick a soul I am
in order to prove how pure a soul you are.
I do not want to go on discussing with you
the cramped feeling that I know nothing,
with you who understand everything,
to whom everything is clear.
Because none of my confessions go to your heart,
they go straight to your cold head.
You take what a friend says
as a statement.
You take a friend's tears
as charges.
You have only one mold but
my aspirations and wounds are countless in number.
so that I cannot approach you now.

A Bureaucrat

He is diligent and sincere.
He comes to work early in the morning,
stays working in solitude until late at night.
He always emphasizes
that he can leave whenever he likes.

A wise fellow, he is on his guard
against anyone who dreams unreasonable dreams.
He scorns inflammatory remarks,
a realist wielding fiercely the scalpel of practicality
he cannot stand companions who lack decorum,
cannot stand uninformed ignorance.
He does all he can to open up the blood vessels
of organizations suffering from hardened arteries.
Sometimes he is the switch awaking sleeping groups,
the tough spanner that tightens all that is loose.
If it's up to him, he even forgives corrupt organizations.

Such a venerable comrade has long been
in the upper levels of our movement. When impure
words and actions come up against his uprightness, they are crushed.
The sounds of infinitely crooked realities are blocked by his decency.
Before his square logic armed with historical perspectives
the intense fury of those who know nothing is lulled,
impatience that knows nothing of the situation is calmly controlled,
disorganized outpourings that do not follow
organizational guidelines and discipline are crushed.

Everything shoddy is managed and administered
by him with smoothness and style,
good manners, in due order, systematically,
he is truly a bureaucrat for today.

Accurate and straight like a second-hand,
it takes a really long time
to know him well.
If you intend to take to the streets and public squares
now, you have to convince him first.

Nothing Goes First

After being deceived by time a number of times
I've got used to it. When I start to feel
that a season has lasted too long,
that moment is the tenderest green
and whenever I felt inclined to give up,
saying that there's no way out in sight, not even the size of a needle's eye,
behind my back another wilderness world was approaching.

Let's not let ourselves be deceived twice.
When you feel like putting an end to your life
that is summer time, opportunity time
telling you to blossom most beautifully.
Love never comes as something elderly.
Even if only a single day remains
still we can grow sincere again.

Bibimbap for Revolutionary Transformation

After working until late
sometimes I go out for a drink on my own.
Feeling rather peckish by then,
there are times when rice serves as a snack.
Today, lacking side dishes,
I just mix in some spinach and old kimchi.
It tastes like honey.
Oh, I never experienced a taste like it!

Then I recall what I have been reading about so closely for so long,
the controversy regarding the transformation of Korean society.
After NL (National Liberation) met up with PD (People's Democracy),
might they have tasted this sweet if mixed together,
neither losing its own taste?
We called the revolution a blast furnace,
so why were we so afraid of being mixed together
and being born as something new?

The reason why we refused to let ourselves be mixed together
was simply the greed of those whose stomachs were full.
Looking from the standpoint of those who are hungry,
nothing makes sense.
What about trying to make something new:
mixing together again NL and PD or whatever
to produce one bibimbap of revolutionary transformation
that will truly become the blood and bone of ordinary people?

That thought,
makes me feel hungrier,
strongly convinced
that I must grow more ardent.

In Praise of Life Outside the Law

It's a strange world, where everyone is frantically insisting
they are going to subject themselves to the law
while the state is boldly telling everyone they must live outside of the law.
Even today, echoes of candlelight protests on City Hall Plaza
condemning the NIS for illegal elections are being driven outside of the law,
the groans of those being driven over the boundary for the maintenance of order
from Gangjeong, from Miryang, can be heard clearly.

Taking nine dismissals as a pretext,
sixty thousand members of the teachers' union are being driven outside of the law,
taking things written on a bulletin board as a pretext,
a hundred thousand civil servants are being driven outside of the law,
taking some kind of meetings as an excuse
a political party legitimate for 20 years is being excluded from the law,
and there have also been farmers excluded from the IMF treaty,
street vendors driven outside of the street-cleaning law
who hanged themselves from streetside trees,
residents evicted under the new-town law
who were burned to death at the top of a watchtower.
The privatization law designed to turn state-owned companies into
    private property,
be it the railways, gas, or medicine,
the irregular workers at Cort Cortek or Hyundai Motors,
where even a supreme court ruling was useless,
another the workers at Ssangyong Motors, Hanjin Heavy Industries,
    Kiryung Electronics
where even the social agreements concluded in the National Assembly
    were disregarded,
this is the period when, every two years, ten million non-regular workers
were driven outside of the law,
a paradise of people living outside of the law
that you can only get free of by giving up your life.

Who on earth can live inside of such laws nowadays?
Now that everyone has been driven outside of the law, inside that law
today, who is safe, who is happy, who is laughing?
Fine! We'll not try to go back inside

that cramped law. We'll not desperately exert ourselves
to go back inside that obscene law of a minority.
Instead. let's make another world outside of the law.
Let's be grateful that what this great nation
has desperately been trying to drive away
is the coming day we've been waiting for for so long.

We Are All the Sewol Ferry

Don't beat about the bush.
The whole of society was the Sewol Ferry.
Capital and power had already removed the ballast
from our lives. Abolishing regular employment
they injected the instability of irregular employment.
They abolished "safety" from every part of society
and replaced it with "greed for unlimited profit."
In the midst of serial disasters of capital, every day seven people
sank regularly in the name of industrial accidents,
in the name of despair about earning a living,
many workers and poor people ran aground on their own.

On the vast deck of this Sewol Ferry age
only capital was infinitely safe, a fully-fed world.
The structural changes made for profit
were always covered by law, while all the unprofitable tasks related to safety
    or peace
or equality were outsourced. In any time of managerial crisis
it was always legitimate for captain-capitalists to abandon their ship
while the SOS signals of the workers who only wished to live together
were sold off and repressed as illegal.
Risks were only transferred further and further down.
People's lives were lost
in that cruel sea of survival.

Yet still they tell us to be quiet,
Not to beat about the bush.
This whole structure must be condemned,
the overall structures of society must be changed.
We have to change the captain and crew of this Republic of Korea
who think only of escaping from this terrible Sewol Ferry time.
We all must come forward and take over as captain,
chief engineer, deckhands, helmsman of this sinking ship.
We all must come forward, urgently take over as the age's last remaining ballast,
air pockets, diving bells.
We have to change the course of this Sewol Ferry age.
We have to change the course of capital.

99% Versus 1%

A street-vendor in Greece,
fifteen-year-old Alexandros,
was killed by a bullet shot by the police.
Red flowers bloomed throughout Greece.

In Tahrir Square, Egypt
Ahmed Harara walked about wearing
an eye-patch inscribed January 29,
the day he lost one eye.
Now he sits there with a patch over the other eye,
inscribed November 20, the day he lost the other eye.

The gales of unemployment having affected
twenty-eight-year-old David in Madrid, Spain,
he sent his CV by mail
to 200 European companies
and in Korea a migrant worker from Vietnam failed the naturalization test
because she could not sing the second verse of the National Anthem.

On Wall Street, the heart of multinational finance
the Occupy movement arose,
99% against 1%,
and across the globe in 1,500 cities in 80 countries
international collective action was organized

With my neck and leg injured
I'm stuck in a Korean prison
in a solitary cell, unable to meet anyone, yet
somehow I don't feel that I'm living alone.

Butterfly Effect

After US forces invaded Iraq,
finally, the truth about the biochemical weapons
they claimed Iraq possessed was revealed. That
was a thousand times stronger than the radioactive
depleted uranium ammunition used by US forces.
Deadly biological and chemical agents, dying children,
dying mothers and fathers, coming out onto the streets,
anti-war waves in favor of peace all over the world
became guided missiles carrying those nukes.
Those weapons that could be found everywhere were not in Iraq.
They had not received Hussein's support.
They were on the streets of Manhattan, New York, the heart of the
    United States.
They were on the lawn in front of Korea's National Assembly
as it was deciding to send troops to Iraq
and also in the heart of the US soldier
who hurled a grenade at his comrades

Those weapons were incredibly weak,
relying on conventional explosives, but
as they used the throbbing hearts of human beings as primers
they covered the inhabited world more powerfully than any
nuclear umbrella,
while they did no damage
but pierced the ears of the world, broke heads,
broke hearts with the words, Mother, Father, Child.
Even after the war was over, still the US could not find
the biochemical weapons they claimed Iraq possessed.
No cutting-edge radar information satellites
will be able to locate the whereabouts
of all those fearsome lives proliferating
in the direction of human dignity. The globalization
that imperialism has tried to establish with the use of shells
we will establish with the very old-fashioned conventional weapons
known as love and compassion.

I Am Not Korean

On January 2, 2014,
in front of the factory of the Korean company 'Yakjin Trading Company'
in the Canadia Industrial Park southwest of Phnom Penh in Cambodia,
about a hundred garment-making workers were merrily dancing.
as they demanded a wage increase.
127 factories were on strike demanding a rise in the minimum wage.

Workers from other Korean businesses in the park were dancing,
Pirun, a worker from 'International Fashion Royal' was dancing.
Working an average of ten hours per day
making expensive clothes for the rich,
Pirun's monthly income was 130 dollars (US $14),
which included 50 cents per hour of overtime work,
a medical allowance of 5 dollars, and a 5 dollars bonus
plus 5 dollars transportation grant that she would lose
if she failed to arrive by 7 am on even one day.

"I too want to have what they call a 'dream',"
said thirty-one-year-old Pabi,
explaining why she participated in the dancing strike.
She spent 40 dollars per month for a space in a small room
shared by four or five others, and 60 dollars on food,
so after working for ten years all she had left was debts of 200 dollars.
Furthermore, she has to renew every six months or one year as a non-
    regular worker.
In the past two years, 4,000 garment laborers in the Canadia
Industrial Park
had fainted during work due to malnutrition.

The military police who came in ten trucks
started to beat the dancing workers with clubs at 3:30 pm.
The 911 brigade of airborne troops, who occupied part of the site of the
    Yakjin factory,
opened a side door and emerged.
The commander of the 911 brigade was a Yakjin shareholder.
The sound of people screaming as they were dragged away
continued until 3 am the next morning.

The next day, furious Canadia Industrial Park workers
filled the streets from early morning. At 8 in the morning, when
the protesters were within two hundred yards of the Interior Ministry,
gunfire erupted. Five people died,
more than thirty people were wounded. A bullet lodged
in Pirun's right leg. She was taken to hospital
but there were no doctors and the nurses said they could not treat her.
Just then another woman, not involved in the protests, was brought to
      the hospital
in need of CPR, but she was refused treatment too
and died on her way back home. Phok, watching the demonstration
from the roof of his house, was hit in left and right ankles and his right thigh.
A motodop driver, Seron, was shot while waiting for customers.
A pregnant women on her way home from buying fish was also shot.
Angry workers started throwing stones at the hospital.

The Korean Embassy in Cambodia
issued an 'emergency statement' before the bloodshed began, claiming that
if a decisive stand was not taken against "illegal behavior by
      unidentified outsiders"
they were "concerned about negative effects on Korean investment
      in Cambodia."
They called for strong intervention by the Cambodian government
      and politicians.
In Cambodia, in 2012, Korea still surpassed China in investments,
and on January 6 the embassy of Korea, the number one investor in Cambodia,
according to the "public safety information" posted on their official
      Facebook page,
"contacted the Capital Garrison Command calling for necessary measures to
      be taken."
"We have also sent messages to the Cambodian National
      Counterterrorism Commission,
Government agencies such as the Ministry of the Interior, the Justice Ministry,
      the National Police,
demanding their cooperation in assuring the safety of our companies and
      preventing damage to them."
They had quickly convinced the government of Cambodia
"to take this situation seriously and prepare steps for dealing with it rapidly,"

reckoning it was their meritorious service. They even boasted that for the
    Cambodian military
to give special protective measures
was something that applied uniquely to Korean factories.
The government of South Korea was the public sponsor
of the 'Prime Minister's Guard' and the '70 Brigade' of Prime Minister
    Hun Sen,
that led the repression, while former President Lee Myung-bak
was an economic advisor to Prime Minister Hun Sen. In 2011
when the prime minister's guard purchased 28 million dollars' worth of
    armored equipment
the Korean government provided financial support. The Korean Association
    of Garment Makers
comprised of 60 companies moved a little faster after the incident.
They moved the Cambodia Garment Producers Association
to sue Sam Rainsy, the representative of the unified opposition party,
and eight labor unions, for a large sum iin compensation.

At about the same time, on January 9, 2014,
at Youngone Corporation's overseas plant located in Chittagong in
    southern Bangladesh,
the legal minimum wage was raised, so the management reduced
    other allowances,
cutting the total wages, at which angry workers
began spontaneous protest demonstrations.
Youngone Corporation is a large enterprise with 17 factories in Bangladesh
and on that payday the police opened fire,
killing a 20-year-old female worker, Parveen Akhtar,
and injuring dozens more.
The minimum wage increased late the previous year was 5,300 takas, 70
    US dollars,
while before the increase it was 40 US dollars. In April 2011, in a
    tragic incident
at Youngone Corporation the police had already shot and killed three workers,
injuring 250 others.
Elsewhere in Bangladesh in April, 2013,
a garment factory built like a chicken coop collapsed,
crushing 1,235 workers.
On the day of Parveen Akhtar's death in Bangladesh,

at 6:50 a.m. at the construction site for Samsung Electronics' new factory in the
    North of Vietnam,
one worker arrived late for work and went rushing through the gate, for which
members of Samsung's security services beat him and stunned him with
    electronic shock sticks,
at which 4,000 Vietnamese construction workers began a 'riot'
that resulted in a large-scale bloodbath. Vietnamese workers
receive a minimum wage of 120 US dollars.

Yakjin Trading Corporation
have built factories in Cambodia, Vietnam and Indonesia,
where they employ 23,000 multinational workers,
while they have just a small head office in Songpa-gu, Seoul.
They produce clothing to order with brand names like
Banana Republic, Gap, Old Navy, etc..

Youngone Trading
have built factories in Bangladesh and China, El Salvador.
The head office employs 448 Koreans,
while there are 52,530 local employees.
They produce North Face and custom-made Nike etc..

With Samsung,
there is no way of knowing
how many overseas factories they have,
and how many workers they employ.

While waiting for two operations, Pirun
would be unable to dance for a while,
or operate a sewing machine.
After that incident, the only Koreans who visited her
were a few reporters.

Who the devil am I?
I've spent about twenty years snooping around labor movements
in Korea's free export zones.
Surely it's inevitable for declining industries to go bankrupt?
Who the devil am I?
I've spent dozens of years among tears of farewell beside workers

from garment factories, electronics factories that have gone bankrupt, closed or
    transferred overseas.
Who the devil am I?
I've fought, demanding that Kiryung Electronics, who transferred their
    factories to China,
should start up the production line again, giving their female workers
direct employment in regular positions.
Who the devil am I?
I've demanded reinstatement for workers at guitar-making Colt-Coltech
who moved their factories to China and Indonesia after a disguised close-
down.
Who the devil am I?
I fought against Jo Nam-ho, chairman of Hanjin Heavy Industries,
who invested 2 trillion won setting up a shipyard in Subic Bay, Philippines,
    employing 20,000 people.
Who the devil am I?
I'm helpless, at my wits' end,
in the face of laws busily beating gravel
saying that due to management crises everything is a fair layoff and use of non-
    regular workers,
and furthermore, layoffs on account of future business crises must also
    be possible.

Who the devil am I?
I fought hard for the 'large factory democratic union'
that agreed to hire the children of full-time workers as a priority,
for the 'large factory democratic union'
that shut its eyes to the proliferation and the priority layoffs of non-
    regular workers,
for the regular workers of public sector their job security
who can now enjoy passable overseas trips
for the regular worker members of the Korean Confederation of Trade Unions
who now form the majority of Korea's middle class.
Who the devil am I?
Every year I visit Mangwol-dong cemetery, furious about the
    Gwangju massacre,
every year, I visit the national workers' rally
commemorating the anniversary of Jeon Tae-il's death,
still I cannot forget the killing of the Yongsan demolition protestors.
Who the devil am I?

I have been assigned to work for the commemoration of the 1985 Guro
    General Strike,
and am sometimes interviewed about the industrialization of the Guro
    industrial complex.
Who the devil am I?
Here, in this neighborhood where migrant workers are concentrated,
I cannot move because of cheap rents.
On this planet, where 85 of the world's richest people
possess the same wealth as one half of the world's population,
who the devil am I?

I am a Korean.
No, I'm not a Korean.
I am Song Kyung-dong.
No, I am not Song Kyung-dong.
I am Pirun, Pabi, Phok, Seron,
Parveen Akhtar.
Countless names,
countless ignorance, pain, suffering, despair
disgrace, on-looking, waiting, transgressions,
falling again, rising again,
riots across borders, solidarity,
struggle and resistance.

* I felt frustrated because I could not understand why, despite the sacrifices and
struggles of so many people, changes in our society are so slow; I despaired of
our society, tainted with little hegemonies, little unionisms, little partisanships,
little nationalisms; then I heard of the bloodshed in Cambodia and felt obliged
to learn more. (The Korean poem ends with a list of the newspapers and other
sources of the detailed information included in the poem).

Sentence Building

After leaving his truck at the bottom of the hill,
the man in the next room makes his way up a couple of miles across the
    snow in the dark.

After returning home at the end of a day's work erecting greenhouse arches,
the man in the next room groans as he turns his frozen body on the hot
    floor as if frying damp laver.

A few days ago the man in the next room dug up red words hidden in the
    sweet potato field,
and even thinned out the winter cabbage words left over in the
    cabbage field.

The man in the next room empties out the beanstalks, inserts the
    year's periods,
then spreads out to dry pepper marks that have not fully ripened in the
    sunlight one day.

If the man in the next room has free time, he hangs persimmon paragraphs
    in rows under the eaves to dry
and if he has no work to do he hangs long radish-top sentences from the
    washing line in the backyard,

So every day the man in the next room comes back home after firmly
    filling in the world's blanks
and makes groaning sounds every night.

How solid his sentences,
how fresh and refined his style, I wonder.

Copyright

The Korea Copyright Committee
wants me to write something about copyright:
whose life have I sold and how much have I saved?
What percentage does the wife's copyright come to,
since she pays for housekeeping and child care?

When I was new at it, being paid for a text is a luxury
and my hope was to receive just one more request.
Perhaps I was all the time dreaming of generous copyright payments
for the sake of a servile old age,
for a life of sufficiency?

Didn't I see others as copyright?
Didn't I imagine others' misery and sorrow
as a guaranteed chance of copyright?
Why do I have to covet that flower's copyright?
Why do I have to covet that soil's copyright?

In actual fact my life's copyright
does not belong to me.

Liberty

From today on my money shall be maple leaves.
Yellow leaves will be 10,000 won notes, red leaves 5,000 won notes,
and those still marked with dark green bruises
will be thousand won notes.

On reflection, people cut down trees to make paper
and you can discern their mind that prints "money" on the glossiest paper,
or puts a high price tag on all that shines,
so you can recognize the fictions that hang dangling from their bodies.

The sunlight, moonlight, petals, buds
offered by the world ... when I reflect that all this
is the wages I plentifully receive
after having been born on this earth and working hard,
so that even the heart that owns nothing grows broad as autumn.

Once I become the currency of precious life
I can gain the courage to go toward you.

A Free Place

After rain has fallen mournfully all day long,
in the heat of the final fun in a tent for an overnight sit-in
where there's nowhere to sit.

Hey, you over there, come over here, they say,
there's a free place here,
but I don't want to sit down anywhere today.

There is a place for self-immolation,
there is a place for wrist-slashing,
there is a place for repeated hunger-strikes,
there is a place for demonstrating high up in the air,
there is a place to return to after being dragged off and arrested.

A bright fluorescent light has been hung up,
but there's no bright place anywhere.
I have no place to sit down,
even inside my dark heart.

A Clear Mirror

I would like my face to be planed with that carpenter's plane,
leaving it a bit angular and scrawny.
I would like to have knots that can't be picked out by hand to project here
and there
and one large sweet potato
raised up on each dark red calf.

I would like my mind to be swarming with concrete things
instead of weary thoughts.
I would like to be bright like that land
where millions of wild flowers bloom along the roadside,
that after giving and giving still has more to give.

A Closed School Everyone Had Left

He did not wake me when he left.

One afternoon, after late autumn rain,
in front of the teacher's house, small silver beads
hung strung on cobwebs in a tree.

A dog, bored, was biting a duck's head.
Bad bitch, a bitch that bites with its mouth is the dirtiest bitch, I scolded
and kicked its ass.

Mist caught on the mountainside across the valley
lingered on into the third day.

When I wake up there'll be no one there
but that's the same for everyone.

I heard the sound of one more seed
falling from a maple tree.

Lovers

For many years, while I was still wet behind the ears,
I hugged and rolled about
oxygen tanks and LPG tanks.

I held them or shouldered them
into gloomy undergrounds or closed pipes,
even took them a long way up in the air.
Kicked by feet,
resolved to fall and die together,
we've even gone rolling down stairs together.

When feet kicked
at my trusting heart
I longed to hit back with a hammer
if the tap opens or it explodes once,
knowing it's hopeless,
gently soothing myself.

It was a time when I gradually realized
that every kind of vigorous labor, like eating iron,
has a strange addiction.

National Defender

When Kim So-yeon, a non-regular worker at Kiryung Electronics,
stood as the presidential candidate for militant workers,
I could not help
since I was resting far up a mountain.

I said I wondered if I'd stay stuck up this mountain if things got really hard,
only look, once past 5:30 pm it's so dark you can't see anything ahead of you,
at which Moon Jae-hun, who had ever lived as a national defender from his
      youth, said:
For you, the only dark thing in front of you is night.
We are engaged in a struggle where we can't see anything ahead regarding
      political ideas.
That's your problem.

Regardless of whether it was true or not,
he, unlike me with all the places I want to visit here and there,
is constantly 'such a political square.'
I replied, with a long laugh,
that I reckoned he was right.

Garibong Hardware Store

Garibong market, the first visit for a long time,
I meet old friends at the tool display.

Fond of being precise like a tape measure,
good at beating like a hammer,
delving deep into everything like a magnifying glass,
penetrating angular opinions horizontally
aiming at essential points like a drill,
old friends had mingled in an old alley,
and chattered about how they were part of labor movement.

We used to feel that every one of us was special
but in fact, weren't we just a bundle of good tools
within the length of a handcart?
We used to think we were bearing something grandiose
along a rough road but
now, just like the simple talk of Chinese-Korean migrant workers
huddled in this alley instead of us,
playing chess,
the thought comes that they might have been very small things

Old In-bong, who's cut all contact with his family,
Old Kyung-gyu, who still works in the pipe business,
Old Bo-yeol, who continues to make sinks,
I hope each and every one is doing all right.

Since I've been looking for a while,
the man in charge of the display asks what I'm looking for.
Previously, I felt I had a lot of needs—
science and philosophy, beliefs, group lines and theories, and so on,
but I really don't know
with what tools
this cool mind
should be tightened up.

The Place Where I Should Be Sitting

Hwanghak-dong flea market,
street side displays, general stores.

A pair of reading glasses that might have been someone's last eyes,
abacus beads, that have poked from the frame,
a radio that has lost its frequency,
a violin whose former owner's hair must have turned white,
a rusting kettle that has forgotten the time it used to boil
vacantly.

Where Have All Those Cats Gone?

One day in the alley where I live
a few fist-sized kittens made an appearance.
After tearing at plastic garbage bags holding waste food
they went dashing back to the window of a real estate's cellar
where a mother cat and her three kittens had made a nest.

It wasn't only those cats
that had made wretched nests for themselves.
In the house where I live, from cellar to third-story attic nine families
     were living,
all of them migrant workers from faraway countries;
it's not only cats that wander around looking for food.
It's those solitary elderly people with handcarts collecting waste paper,
or that guy in a tracksuit hurriedly picking up cigarette butts from off
     the street,
there's also the fellow in a bongo truck with a loudspeaker
who sells culled hens tough as boots as young chickens,
those guys driving around in trucks selling stale fish, stale vegetables,
     stale fruit,
all of them the same, prowling through Garibong's run-down alleys
in search of a bite to eat.
When wife and kids started to wonder
if we shouldn't give them something to eat, I cut them short,
but it's not just those cats that live like that.
We were born and grew up in this land but our situation
is the same as their's, living as aliens, without so much as one room of our own,
forced to keep moving, paying monthly rent or key money, our situation
is the same as their's, moving from this factory to that,
wandering the streets, laid off, unemployed, homeless non-regular workers,
until I stopped wondering who was most to be pitied.

As I lie there, kept awake till dawn by suchlike worries about life,
as any every day the footsteps of people
going out to their daily work pass by,
while the mewing of the kittens since early morning
sounds like children crying, reminding us they have to keep on living.
Thinking that I should save all the world's young first,

I decide to give the kittens some milk,
take a liter of milk, go out
and fill a plastic bowl to the brim, return home then wonder:
have they already drunk some?
have they drunk some now?.
and until misty day dawns
I keep going out and prowling around.

Smoky Mountain

I follow the valley uphill.
There are lots of chestnuts fallen from the trees.
Even now, 650 million people in the world are hungry.
Every seven seconds one child starves to death.
It is said that seven million people lose their sight every year due
    to malnutrition.
I pick up chestnuts, reluctant to let them go to waste,.

One is for a child panting in a Somalia refugee camp. One is for a child grubbing up grass roots in the wastelands of Sudan, where two million civilians have died in civil war. One is for a mother from a slum in Manila, capital of the Philippines, who spends the day combing through Smoky Mountain, vast mounds of garbage piled up like a mountain. One for a father come to an Ethiopian relief camp begging for help, holding his son on a ragged cloth, his stomach bulging like a spider's. One for the Zambian children who can be saved from famine with the same amount of corn that Californian cattle consume. One for the farmers and their children who cultivate cotton for French textile factories, cacao for British chocolate factories, sugarcane, tea and peanuts for the Western sugar industry, in Chad, Ghana, Tanzania and Burundi, Rwanda, Jamaica, Brazil and Senegal. One for the children in North Korea whose growth is stunted, no need to go very far. One for Chile's Allende, who was killed in a 1973 coup d'état, after planning to distribute 0.5 liters of milk powder each day to all the children under the age of 15. One for the Nicaraguan Sandinista National Liberation Front comrades who were killed by US forces in 1982 for handing out land ownership certificates and rifles to the landless classes to protect their rights. One for the young revolutionary Thomas Sankara of Burkina Faso and his colleagues, the hope of the African landless classes, killed in 1987. . . .

I pick up chestnuts, one by one.
Should I count myself lucky
to live in a country where I can survive without gathering roots and tree bark,
where I can eat at least enough to get by without working too hard?
It is reported that the total assets of 225 of the world's capitalists
amount to more than what 2.5 billion of the world's poor earn in a year,
that the sales of the world's 100 largest conglomerates

amount to more than the total amount earned from exports by 120 of the
    poorest countries,
that the amount of speculative finance capital moving across the world each year
is more than 63 times greater than the value of goods and services
    produced worldwide,
that even without my harvesting anything, the world produces more than
    enough grain
for the needs of everyone.

I lost my way somewhere in history,
I'm wandering alone in a mountain valley,
the sun is setting in the West
and I am picking up chestnuts.
I am picking up myself, who have come flowing from somewhere.
I stoop down once more.

Factories Produce Graves

One more person hanged himself
at the GM Incheon plant.
Not long ago, at the Ssangyong Motors factory in Pyeongtaek
the twenty-fourth person attempted suicide.
The coffin of Choi Gang-seo, who hanged himself in the union office
of Busan Hanjin Heavy Industries, could not easily leave the factory floor,
even though he was dead.
A few days ago, a dump truck driver ended his life
by placing a brazier of burning coals in his car.
They all died because they found life too difficult,
even with cars bigger than elephants,
even making boats thousands of times bigger
than the largest whale in the world,
even assembling a few hundred cars a day
each worth tens of thousands of dollars,
their livelihood was too little.

Stories of strange animals in a strange country—
the more they work, the poorer they become,
they're obsolete before they grow old,
they can't leave the factory
or their livelihood even when they're dead.

A Decade With Kiryung

The agreement approved by the National Assembly was just a scrap of paper,
siphoning off $ 60,000 from a $ 100 million company was above suspicion,
abandoning workers and making a midnight flit was legal,
a daylight visit to the president's home was housebreaking.

Even if you wear mourning dress and carry a coffin,
even if you fast for ninety-four days and make high-up protest sit-ins four times,
even if you shave your head and make thousands of prostrations,
still you're under the yoke as a non-regular worker.

The lesson learned in a decade
with Kiryung Electronics show
that clearly capital has no personality,
that the state is enlisted on the side of those wearing a cloak of legality.

This is a lesson resulting in tears of blood,
not asking if there is no answer
but instead asking if a new answer
isn't needed.

Routes

When grieving family members tried to enter the headquarters
of Samsung Electronics, where leukemia deaths kept increasing,
the security guards told them:
"You mustn't do this. There are plenty of other routes."

After an irregular workers' rally,
they proposed a march to the National Assembly in Yeouido,
at which detectives from the information service of Yeongdeungpo Police
    Station said:
"That is not the promised route."

Then which way should we go
in order to make our voices heard?

Eight Steps

In memory of Song Kuk-hyeon

The door, fitted with automatic sensors,
was wide open
yet he could not get out.
Scorching fire was approaching
but he could not talk
or stand up.

If he had taken only eight steps
he could have gotten out.
He lived in a prison-like isolation facility for twenty-seven years.
He wanted to live with other people
so moved to a self-help home six months before.
His living expenses were 30,000 won per month.
A few days before he had been happy, buying new clothes and shoes.

He went to the Seongdong branch of the National Pension Service
where there was a disability grade review center and begged:
"I need to support for an activity assistant so I can live.
Please raise my disability rating.
re-evaluate me, and even before the result
I need urgent welfare support."
He also went to Seongdong Community Service Center just three
days before.

It was only after he was dead
that he could prove that his disability went beyond third degree
and was close to special level. What a cruel world this is,
in which thirty-five thousand disabled people
have to make desperate efforts
to prove that they are more disabled.

Everyone
can reach another world
if they take just eight steps.

* On April 13, 2014, Song Kuk-hyeon died. Until his death, he was part of
the protest at Gwanghwamun Underground Station demanding the "aboli-
tion of the disability rating system, of obligatory support." All candidates at
the last presidential election promised to abolish this, but the promise has
not been kept to date.

You Must Be Feeling Good

In memory of the death of workers laid off by Ssangyong Motors

You must be feeling good.
Now, you don't need to shoot to death, beat to death, stab to death
with guns and clubs and bayonets
as in Gwangju on May 18,
since they die on their own.

You must be feeling good.
Now, you don't have to push people to their death
like Park Chang-su of Hanjin Heavy Industries
or Kim Kyeong-suk of YH Trading.
They fall to death on their own.

You must be feeling good.
Now, even without enclosing people in a watchtower with no exit
then trampling, burning and killing them
like in Yongsan.
Their blood dries up and they die on their own.

You must be feeling really good..
This state of security over all the land,
this cakewalk, this Bravo,
with the passage of time, money grows on trees,
so happy that your guts burst, your mouth gapes from ear to ear,
you go crazy.

Only workers are drowning in a sea of tears.
A sea of tears, working their fingers to the bone for the rest of their lives,
a sea of tears, wearing themselves out on the streets for the rest of
    their lives,
a sea of tears as finally they put an end to their lives.
You must be feeling good with the workers' world,
nothing but a salty sea of tears.

How to live in this sad world?
Not pressed for by quotas and productivity,
not pursued by the police,
not pressed by unemployment and hardship.

You must be feeling good to precede me to the grave?
Rather, you must be happy to precede me to the grave?
I don't know what to say.

Capital has reached the edge of the cliff
by unlimited competition, unlimited production, unlimited consumption,
so why should we good guys be the only ones pushed over and buried?
How many more people have to be slaughtered
before the crisis of capital is solved?
This is a planned massacre,
capital's terror aimed at our time as a whole.

Without digging up the truth
we cannot bury these twenty-two grim dead bodies.
Without condemning you,
I cannot bear to see the sad eyes of these children.
I cannot write this kind of sad memorial poem again,
I cannot utter this kind of heart-breaking address again.

So let's rise up.
Not dying any more,
let's rise up and fight.

* I wrote this memorial poem when the fifteenth death among the workers fired by Ssangyong Motors in 2011 was announced. We began to hold a weekly memorial festival with workers fired by Ssangyong Motor in front of Bongsingak in Seoul. Lee Chang-geun and Ssangyong automobile workers together with us started the Bus of Hope soon after. Intent on there being not one death like those from Hanjin Heavy Industries, it went repeatedly to Busan. In 2012, I was released from prison on bail and had just come out of hospital after another operation on my leg when news came of the twenty-second Ssangyong Motors victim. An altar was set up at the gate of Deoksu Palace, a national commission of enquiry was formed, and again I joined in. By the end of 2013, President Park had still not keep her promise of a government enquiry, while the number of victims rose to twenty-eight. I have had to read this poem several times, revising the number of deaths each time.

The Workers' National Flag

In honor of the martyr Jin Gi-seung

On April 30, 2014, at 11 pm,
one hour before the 124th Anniversary of Workers' Day began,
Jin Gi-seung, a worker laid off by Shinsung Passenger Company in Jeonju,
tried to hang himself from the flagstaff for the Korean national flag
placed above the company entrance.

The company identified itself with the state,
its president identified himself with a sovereign.
National competitiveness being the same as corporate competitiveness,
employees were obliged to recite the pledge and salute the flag
every morning.

After he was arrested during the strike,
he saw the national flag hanging right in front
of the police station, the holding cells, the lawcourt.
And when he went to appeal against unfair dismissal
at the local Labor Relations Commission, the National Labor
    Relations Commission,
the Administrative Tribunal, there, too, hung the national flag.

Perhaps you wanted to declare:
See, this is not our national flag.
This is not the workers' national flag. Today is the day
when, loosening that tight noose,
you will go back to heaven, where there are no more bonds,
only a day when the tears and pain
from too much death
have all been wiped away.

* On April 30, 2014, Jin Gi-seung hanged himself from the company's flag-staff for the National Flag, leaving a note urging others not to let themselves be dismissed unfairly but to exercise their rights, He had received an under-taking that if he knelt in front of the company's president asking for forgive-ness he would be reinstated. He did so, but still was not reinstated. Instead,

after his character was defamed he hanged himself, and on the day following that, the administrative court of first instance declared his dismissal to be null and void. On May 19, the company appealed that verdict although he was brain dead. On June 2, he finally died, and on July 22, 51 days later that, his funeral was held as a National Democratic Workers' Funeral in Pungnam-mun Square in Jeonju and then moved to Mangwol-dong Cemetery in Gwangju. At that time, some May group members tried to prevent him from being buried in Mangwol-dong cemetery, saying 'there had to be standards.' They reasoned that the workers' struggle was not a democratization movement but a struggle for the right to live. A fight broke out and the police arrested two people. That was an even sadder day

Our Christmas

Thinking of Samsung Electronics irregular worker-martyr Choi Jong-beom's daughter 'Star'

Is there a road that leads to heaven?
Is there a road that leads straight there?
Can I get a ticket if I go to that Catholic church with its red ivy?
Will it be enough to go to that imposing fortress-like Protestant church
    and wait?

Can ten million irregulars go in as regulars?
Can a laid-off worker kicked out of the factory go in without a pass?
Can those evicted, and street vendors too who keep getting carted off,
and immigrant workers, too, get in easily without discrimination?

Is there a road that leads to heaven?
They say Heaven's a good place,
but do they practice real-estate speculation there?
If so, common folk like us won't be able to go.

Is that road also blocked by police buses in rows?
Is that road too controlled by government power?
Are hired thugs camped along that road, too?

Without having to hang myself,
douse myself in oil, without gassing myself with a coal-briquette,
or climbing up a watchtower or pylon and jumping off,
is there a road that leads to heaven?

I mean to say,
without picking up stones again,
without forming scrums again,
is there a road that leads to heaven?

* "Working at a Samsung service center is too difficult. Too hungry to go
on living, everyone was having such a hard time that I cannot bear to look
at them. So even though I cannot burn myself to death like Jeon Tae-il, I've

made my choice. I only hope it will help." On October 31, 2013, Choi Jong-beom, who had been working at the Cheonan Samsung Electronics service center committted suicide with gas from a burning coal briquette. It was just a few days before the first birthday of his baby daughter Star. To this day, Samsung, that so-called leading company, employs some ten thousand service engineers in its 160 service centers, all of them on an irregular basis without basic rights.

To Myself Who Can Still Speak

For the 25th anniversary of martyr Mun Song-myeon

Yesterday I told my child about you.

I told him how, in 1987, there was a boy fifteen years old, like he is now.
Born in Seosan, South Chungcheong Province
he went to work in a factory making mercury in Yeongdeungpo,
believing their promise that he could attend school in the evenings.
By the end of two months, his hands and feet were paralyzed,
dizzy, he kept falling down.
No one knew the name of the disease until finally,
at Seoul National University Hospital, mercury poisoning was diagnosed.
He had to wait several months for it to be recognized as an industrial accident.
Once recognized, he was transferred to Yeouido St. Mary's Hospital,
then, three days after the transfer, he died.
Soon after the boy died, in Guri city,
among workers at Wonjin rayon, cases of occupational disease appeared,
this time it was carbon disulfide poisoning.
The fight was long, lasting some ten years
but the recognized cases alone came to over a thousand
so that at the end of the fight, a hospital specializing in industrial accidents
    was established,
Green Hospital where I was later hospitalized, together with workers from
Kiryung Electronics, Colt-Coltech, Samsung Semiconductors,
    Ssangyong Motors,
so his dad benefitted from Mun Song-myeon's death,
and a lot of people were found eligible for industrial accident benefits.
All thanks to one boy's death.
"Therefore I've decided to recite a memorial poem.
Would you like to go with me?"

Just then, my child said he needed new summer sandals
so I took him to a newly opened mall, built
on the site of Daewoo Apparel, where the Guro general strike started,
and I told him that story, too.

In 1985, there was a garment factory here, called Daewoo Apparel.
while Mario Outlet over there, diagonally opposite, was the site of
    Hyosung Products.
The women working here
startred the first workers' general strike after Liberation.
Aged fourteen or fifteen, they had to pick out scraps of thread
and handle scissors larger than their own hands.
Veteran workers were in their mid-twenties,
the dormitories were like barracks, they were forbidden to go outside.
They lived crammed together, several in each tiny room they called
    Chicken Village.
Fifty were arrested, two thousand were fired.
The library you often visit is on the place
that used to be the Eunil girls' vocational high school,
where young women workers with sleepy eyes
attended special classes for industry.

On our way out after buying summer sandals and a nice wallet
we happened to come out through the back door.
There was another memorable building over there.
You see that three-story building?
That's where your Dad and Mom met,
at the Guro Workers' Literary Society.
Your Dad and Mom lived here for ten year when we were young.

All those places erased now under the shadow of capital.
As we headed home along the road, briefly moving,
briefly cooling,
I kept thinking of you.
Tomorrow, when I go to visit you, what should I say?
Should I make empty compliments about how, because of you, life grew
    safer for many?
Should I not mention revolution any longer
but denounce our poverty, now that we are adicted to everyday comforts.
Should I confess my youth's passion,
grown chill and cold now, like mercury?
I'll say I don't know what to do about this world, so complicated now.
I'll say that if I worry even just a little, it's as though my head will burst,
the circuits are tangled, it drives me crazy.

Should I confess my dying reason?
What should I say? Should I inject this wretched world
with the lethal drug of competition,
consume hallucinogens of consumption every day,
suck up and swallow the mercury of unemployment,
inhale the carbon disulfide of non-regular work,
swallow the organic solvents of layoffs for restructuring,
swallow the poison of soaring rentals, key money, tuition,
after suffering here like gadflies
with no way out,
with no ventilation,
obliged to swallow the final comfort we call suicide
by slow burning coals, hanging or falling,
what should I say about this age of the everyday death of so many people,
that vast mass of desires proliferating continuously, unlimited, today,
on such miserable human families
known as profit, known as capital, known as power?

What should we say.
not to you who are without words
but to myself who can still speak,
not to you who went away after giving all life to us,
but to those children who still have long to live?
I go and peep from time to time into my child's bedroom
where, with sandals and wallet laid beside the bed,
he's dreaming some good dream,
soon to be forgotten, giggling, talking in his sleep,
while I write a poem for you,
a poem that can never really be written,
for you who, like Oskar Matzerath in *The Tin Drum*, will never grow older.

Evening Playground

Children go flying about
like black plastic bags. Old folks saunter along, too,
enjoying the day's last sunlight.
A child crying at having lost its folded dump card
is being dragged home by its mother.
Night comes plodding along the newly made road
in full dress. The childrens' eyes grow dim,
incline more and more towards the ground. At such moments
one small new grave emerges on the playground. I long to hug it
but a larger darkness languishes within me.
White mourning ribbons pinned in the night sky,
stars set off on calls of condolence.

Additional Credits

The following poems were also published in *Korean Literature Now* Vol. 41 Autumn 2018

The Air Club
The Sea's Interrogation Room
The Day I Learned a Lesson
99% Versus 1%
Our Christmas

About the Author

Song Kyeong-dong is a major Korean participatory poet and resistance activist. He has published five poetry collections: *Kkuljam* (*Honey Sleep*), *Sasohan mureumdeure dapham* (*Answers to Small Questions*), *Naneun Hangugini anida* (*I Am Not Korean*), *Naeil dasi sseugesseupnida* (*I Will Write Again Tomorrow*), and *Kkumkkuneun sori hago jappajyeossne* (*I Made a Dreaming Sound and Fell Asleep*). He has also published a prose collection *Kkum kkuneun ja japhyeoganda* (*The Dreamer Is Arrested*). He has received numerous literary awards, including the Shin Dong-yeop Literary Award, the Gosan Literary Award, the Cheon Sang-byeong Literary Award, and the Jo Tae-il Literary Award. He was also selected for two awards given to social activists. He was an invited poet at the Brooklyn Book Festival held in New York, USA, in 2018.

He has been involved in many major labor and social movements in Korea for the past twenty years, including the Committee Against the Expansion and Relocation of the US Military Base in Pyeongtaek, the Committee for the Sewol Ferry Disaster, the Action for the Resignation of President Park Geun-hye, the Committee for the Reinstatement of Ssangyong Motors Dismissed Workers, and the Culture and Arts Blacklist Truth Investigation Committee. In 2011, he was arrested for leading the Hope Bus movement, a movement against neoliberal restructuring.

As of 2024, in addition to his creative activities, he is working as a committee member for various activist groups and a standing director of Ikcheon Cultural Foundation, Gildongmu.

About the Translator

Brother Anthony was born in 1942 in England. He completed his studies in Medieval & Modern Languages at Oxford, then joined the Community of Taizé (France) in 1969. Since 1980, he has been living in Korea. He is now an Emeritus Professor in the English Department at Sogang University.

He has published over seventy volumes of English translations of modern Korean literature, including including Park Nohae's "Dawn of Labor" and other poetic works by Kim Seung-Hee, Lee Si-young, Sin Yong-mok, and many others. He was awarded the Korean Government's Order of Cultural Merit in 2008. He took Korean citizenship in 1994. In December 2015 he was awarded an honorary MBE by Queen Elizabeth. He recently received the 2024 Manhae Award for Literature. His home page is at http://anthony.sogang.ac.kr/

Free Verse Editions

Edited by Jon Thompson

13 ways of happily by Emily Carr
& in Open, Marvel by Felicia Zamora
& there's you still thrill hour of the world to love by Aby Kaupang
Alias by Eric Pankey
the atmosphere is not a perfume it is odorless by Matthew Cooperman
At Your Feet (A Teus Pés) by Ana Cristina César, edited by
    Katrina Dodson, trans. by Brenda Hillman and Helen Hillman
Bari's Love Song by Kang Eun-Gyo, translated by Chung Eun-Gwi
Between the Twilight and the Sky by Jennie Neighbors
Blade Work by Lily Brown
Blood Orbits by Ger Killeen
The Bodies by Christopher Sindt
The Book of Isaac by Aidan Semmens
The Calling by Bruce Bond
Canticle of the Night Path by Jennifer Atkinson
Child in the Road by Cindy Savett
Civil Twilight by Giles Goodland
Condominium of the Flesh by Valerio Magrelli, trans. by Clarissa Botsford
Contrapuntal by Christopher Kondrich
Country Album by James Capozzi
Cry Baby Mystic by Daniel Tiffany
The Curiosities by Brittany Perham
Current by Lisa Fishman
Day In, Day Out by Simon Smith
Dear Reader by Bruce Bond
Dismantling the Angel by Eric Pankey
Divination Machine by F. Daniel Rzicznek
Elsewhere, That Small by Monica Berlin
Empire by Tracy Zeman
Erros by Morgan Lucas Schuldt
Extinction of the Holy City by Bronisław Maj, trans. by Daniel Bourne
Fifteen Seconds without Sorrow by Shim Bo-Seon, trans. by
    Chung Eun-Gwi and Brother Anthony of Taizé
The Forever Notes by Ethel Rackin
The Flying House by Dawn-Michelle Baude
General Release from the Beginning of the World by Donna Spruijt-Metz